The Mermaids

# of Jamaica

OTHER TITLES IN THE COLLECTION

Written by
CLAUDIA BELLANTE

Illustrated by
HERIKITA

The Mermaids

# of Jamaica

Crocodile Books, USA
An imprint of Interlink Publishing Group, Inc.
www.interlinkbooks.com

To Tina, my cool little mermaid, and my Flor,
who called me that for the first time during
those happy Cuban times.

Claudia

. . . .

For Ágatha and all the girls born with a
strength against all odds, like that of a shoot of
grass growing between the pavement.

Herikita

First American edition published 2023 by
CROCODILE BOOKS
An imprint of Interlink Publishing Group, Inc.
46 Crosby Street, Northampton, Massachusetts 01060
www.interlinkbooks.com

Library of Congress Cataloging-in-Publication Data available
ISBN 978-1-62371-792-6 • hardback

Printed and bound in China on forest-friendly paper
10 9 8 7 6 5 4 3 2 1

Against All Odds was born out of the desire to tell our kids real stories of children living in distant places and facing unique situations.

The series talks about everyday gestures that in certain contexts can become important, even to the point of changing the course of events, defying prejudices and clichés, and redirecting our attention to often-overlooked problems.

All of the events described in these books really happened or are currently happening. Only the protagonists are the result of the poetic license; the author wanted to protect the identities of the minors involved in these stories.

There is an island in the heart of the Caribbean, covered by lush jungle and surrounded by an ocean full of fish and corals. On this island the houses are colorful, and there are large collective taxis loaded with people.

A radio is always playing songs that say "Sun is shining, the weather is sweet" or "One love, one heart. Let's get together and feel all right."

It's Jamaica! The island of Bob Marley, the reggae singer with long dreadlocks, and the island where a group of young mermaids live.

They have the names of warriors, like Ketana, which means "house," or Kamoya, "judge," but they did not come out of a fairy tale, they are not the daughters of Poseidon, they do not dwell at the bottom of the sea, and they do not have long tails covered in scales.

Because Ketana and Kamoya, along with their eight companions, are normal girls who study and eat ice cream, but they're also capable of something rare and wonderful: spinning around in the water like butterflies in the sky.

Together they form the only synchronized swimming team in the small coastal town of Port Antonio and in all of Jamaica, but being representatives of their country requires hard work and sacrifice.

Every day after school, when the bell rings to mark the end of classes, the girls close their books and run to the top of the hill. Once there, they dive like dolphins into the crystal-clear water of a pool with infinity views .

Olga, their coach, comes from Moscow and has competed in three Olympic Games, winning two gold medals. She is tall, blonde, and seemingly strict, but she has a tender smile that lights up her face every time her young swimmers nail the choreography. She started swimming as a child. Her mother would accompany her to the pool and urge her to do better.

She was brought up firmly and harshly, but when she arrived in Jamaica and met her students, she realized she needed a different strategy to earn their trust.

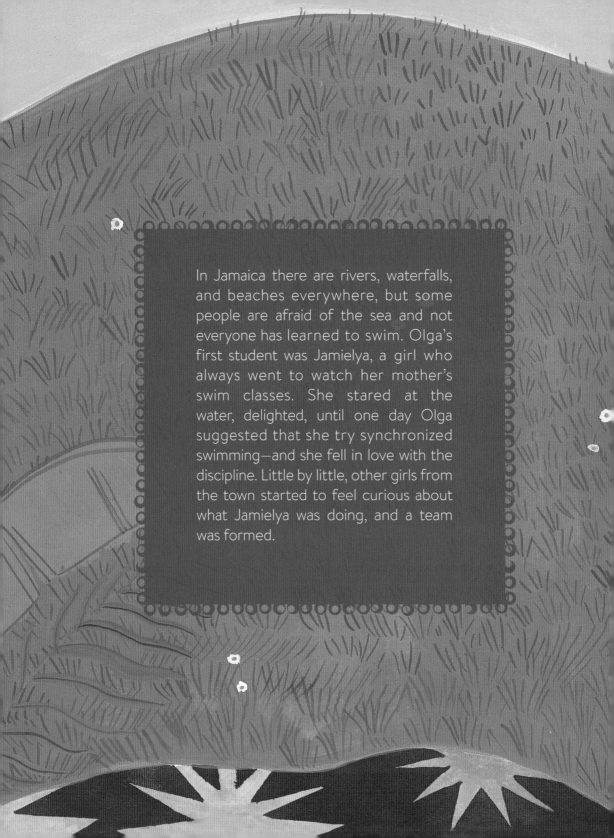

In Jamaica there are rivers, waterfalls, and beaches everywhere, but some people are afraid of the sea and not everyone has learned to swim. Olga's first student was Jamielya, a girl who always went to watch her mother's swim classes. She stared at the water, delighted, until one day Olga suggested that she try synchronized swimming—and she fell in love with the discipline. Little by little, other girls from the town started to feel curious about what Jamielya was doing, and a team was formed.

Olga requires commitment and concentration from the girls because a great adventure awaits them this summer: they will go to China for two months, with qualified trainers at their disposal to learn from and improve their skills. It's a unique opportunity that could change their future, and they must be ready for it.

Some of the older students who attended the previous year said it was very hard and that they didn't have a moment to rest, but they also talked about trying new foods and seeing new sights. The little ones are excited, and some have even learned to count in Chinese.

Calsia in particular is very happy. She's always loved the ballet called *Swan Lake* and will finally get classical dance training in China.

Olga's students are between seven and eighteen years old. The older ones take care of the younger ones, help them with choreography, and are very strict. The sport has led them to become close friends, and in the locker room, they share their dreams and secrets.

Water is Ajoni's calling; she loves scuba diving and wants to be a biologist.

Julicia wants to be a pilot, but she never goes to the sea because she's afraid of the waves carrying her away. Ketana loves the Harry Potter books, and Micah wants to be a math teacher. Kamoya has a beautiful voice, like all mermaids, and a sweet face. She earned third place in a beauty contest on the same day that she won a synchro competition. That day, she believed anything was possible.

Practice lessons have a price, and it also costs money to get to the pool and back home.

As if that weren't difficult enough, many Jamaican women become mothers very young and are forced to give up their ambitions.

But for the mermaids of Port Antonio, synchronized swimming is a magical antidote to all this and the water in which they're submerged helps protect them and keep them from growing up too soon.

To prepare for the journey to China, Olga has asked the girls to focus on their goals by writing on a blackboard how they plan to achieve them and in how much time.

Joydayne wrote that she wants learn to control her nerves and anxiety so that she can perform her favorite move flawlessly. It's called barracuda, and it requires going from a horizontal position to a vertical one, with legs stretched out like spaghettis.

Nyouka has promised that she'll watch more videos of choreography and will work to improve her endurance.

Nishtoy will eat more fruits and vegetables and dream of winning a gold medal.

Since they started training, Olga tries to get the girls to participate in as many competitions as possible and organizes shows at the hotels on the island, where the crowds always watch in astonishment.

On those occasions, they wear bright, colorful bathing suits and get to choose the soundtrack for their choreographies.

The girls' parents trust Olga and are convinced that swimming is teaching their daughters discipline and the importance of helping each other in times of need.

The day before the big trip, the girls are impatient. Olga has brought new team uniforms, with the name of each member on the backs of the sweatshirts. Parents have organized a party with chicken and pies, and when they think about what awaits their daughters, the emotion makes them teary-eyed.

The young mermaids of Port Antonio have come much further than they could've ever imagined, not with scaly tails or spells, but thanks to friendship and commitment. Diving courageously and dancing underwater to their own beat, they have built their future swimming against the current.

AUTHOR'S NOTE

I visited the small town of Port Antonio after reading about Olga Novokshchenova's team, Port Antonio Synchro, in the *New York Times* and immediately falling in love with the story.

When I was little and did classical dance, I watched Esther Williams movies and always thought synchronized swimming seemed like a magical discipline that required endurance and grace at the same time.

When I visited, I learned that Jamaica is a beautiful and complex island facing many challenges. Many girls become mothers very young and families are often separated because many must emigrate to find work.

I spent 48 hours at the edge of the pool, observing the movements of these amazing young mermaids and talking to them every time they went out for a break. I met their parents; most were people with modest jobs that have now become part of an extended family.

Olga says that she is just a coach to the girls, but she is much more than that. I was there on the day she held the preparatory meeting for the imminent trip to China, and at the end of the meeting there was a party. The parents brought food and had prepared a gift for Olga.

One by one, they thanked her and hugged her. Kamoya, the girl with a beautiful voice, sang a famous Mariah Carey song whose words could not be more apt: "And then a hero comes along / With the strength to carry on / And you cast your fears aside / And you know you can survive / So when you feel like hope is gone / Look inside you and be strong / And you'll finally see the truth / That a hero lies in you."